Dinosaurs

Tyrannosaurus Rex

Daniel Nunn

Heinemann Library
Chicago, Illinois

© 2007 Heinemann Library
a division of Reed Elsevier Inc.
Chicago, Illinois

Customer Service 888-454-2279
Visit our website at www.heinemannraintree.com

Designed by Joanna Hinton-Malivoire
Printed and bound in China by South China Printing Co. Ltd.

11 10 09 08 07
10 9 8 7 6 5 4 3 2 1

The Library of Congress has cataloged the first edition of this book as follows:
Nunn, Daniel.
  Tyrannosaurus rex / Daniel Nunn.
     p. cm. -- (Dinosaurs)
  Includes bibliographical references and index.
  ISBN-13: 978-1-4034-9444-3 (library binding - hardcover)
  ISBN-13: 978-1-4034-9451-1 (pbk.)
  1. Tyrannosaurus rex--Juvenile literature. I. Title.
  QE862.S3N865 2007
  567.912'9--dc22
                           2006030060

Acknowledgements
The publishers would like to thank the following for permission to reproduce photographs: Alamy pp. 11 (Mike Danton), 22 (www.white-windmill.co.uk); Corbis pp. 7 (Zefa/Peter Adams), 9 and 23 (Royalty-Free); 16 (Charles Platiau/Reuters), 19, 22 and 23 (Philip Gould), 21 (Craig Lovell); Istock p. 20 (DoctorBass); Science Photo Library pp. 9 (Mark Garlick), 18 (Carlos Goldin).

Cover photograph of Tyrannosaurus rex reproduced with permission of Alamy/Mike Danton.

Contents

The Dinosaurs

Dinosaurs were reptiles.

Dinosaurs lived long ago.

Tyrannosaurus rex was a dinosaur.

Tyrannosaurus rex lived long ago.

Today there are no
Tyrannosaurus rex.

Tyrannosaurus Rex

Velociraptor

Some dinosaurs were small.

But *Tyrannosaurus rex* was big.

Tyrannosaurus rex had strong legs.

Tyrannosaurus rex walked on two feet.

Tyrannosaurus rex had short arms.

Tyrannosaurus rex had a long tail.

Tyrannosaurus rex had sharp teeth.

Tyrannosaurus rex had a
strong jaw.

Tyrannosaurus rex had a big head.

Tyrannosaurus rex ate
other dinosaurs.

How Do We Know?

Scientists have found fossils
of *Tyrannosaurus rex*.

Fossils are parts of animals that lived long ago.

fossil

Fossils are in rocks.

Fossils tell us what *Tyrannosaurus rex* was like.

Fossil Quiz

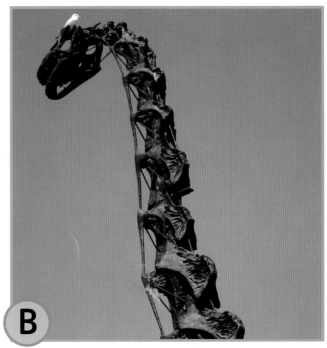

One of these fossils was *Tyrannosaurus rex*. Can you tell which one?

Picture Glossary

 **dinosaur** an animal that lived long ago

 **fossil** parts of a dead animal that lived long ago

 **reptile** animal that is cold-blooded. Snakes, lizards, turtles, and alligators are reptiles.

Answer to question on page 22
Fossil A was *Tyrannosaurus rex*.
Fossil B was *Brachiosaurus*.

Index

Notes to Parents and Teachers

This series gives a first introduction to dinosaurs. In simple language, each book explains the physical characteristics of different dinosaurs, their behavior, and how fossils have provided a key into our knowledge of dinosaurs' existence and extinction. An expert was consulted to provide both interesting and accurate content. The text has been carefully chosen with the advice of a literacy expert to ensure that beginners can read the text independently or with moderate support.

You can support children's nonfiction literacy skills by helping students use the table of contents, picture glossary, and index.